Tales From Anywhere

Two One-Act Plays

by Megan Orr

Single copies of plays are sold for reading purposes only. The copying or duplicating of a play, or any part of play, by hand or by any other process, is an infringement of the copyright. Such infringement will be vigorously prosecuted

Baker's Plays
7611 Sunset Blvd.
Los Angeles, CA 90042
BAKERSPLAYS.COM

NOTICE

This book is offered for sale at the price quoted only on the understanding that, if any additional copies of the whole or any part are necessary for its production, such additional copies will be purchased. The attention of all purchasers is directed to the following: This work is protected under the copyright laws of the United States of America, in the British Empire, including the Dominion of Canada, and all other countries adhering to the Universal Copyright Convention. Violations of the Copyright Law are punishable by fine or imprisonment, or both. The copying or duplication of this work or any part of this work, by hand or by any process, is an infringement of the copyright and will be vigorously prosecuted.

This play may not be produced by amateurs or professionals for public or private performance without first submitting application for performing rights. Royalties are due on all performances whether for charity or gain, or whether admission is charged or not Since performance of this play without the payment of the royalty fee renders anybody participating liable to severe penalties imposed by the law, anybody acting in this play should be sure, before doing so, that the royalty fee has been paid. Professional rights, reading rights, radio broadcasting, television and all mechanical rights, etc. are strictly reserved. Application for performing rights should be made directly to BAKER'S PLAYS.

No one shall commit or authorize any act or omission by which the copyright of, or the right to copyright, this play may be impaired. No one shall make any changes in this play for the purpose of production.

Publication of this play does not imply availability for performance. Both amateurs and professionals considering a production are strongly advised in their own interest to apply to Baker's Plays for written permission before starting rehearsals, advertising, or booking a theatre.

Whenever the play is produced, the author's name must be carried in all publicity, advertising and programs. Also, the following notice must appear on all printed programs, "Produced by special arrangement with Baker's Plays."

Licensing fees for *TALES FROM ANYWHERE* is based on a per performance rate and payable one week in advance of the production.
Please consult the Baker's Plays website at www.bakersplays.com or our current print catalogue for up to date licensing fee information.

Copyright © 2008 by Megan Orr
Made in U.S.A. All rights reserved.

TALES FROM ANYWHERE
ISBN 978-0-87440-304-6   #1811-B

TWICE UPON A TIME

CHARACTERS
(2/3M, 4W, Extras)

(In order of appearance)

PRINCESS CHRISTINA CARLYLE - Age 17; a junior at the Academy; beautiful, blonde, superficial, stuck-up, flirtatious

PRINCESS RENEE RICHARDS - Age 16; a sophomore at the Academy; CHRISTINA's shadow; cute, petite brunette

PRINCESS LYNN LEONARDO - Age 17; a junior at the Academy; AIDEN's best friend; outspoken, opinionated, optimistic

PRINCESS AIDEN ALEXANDER - Age 17; a junior at the Academy; pretty, friendly, well-rounded

*****PRINCE SHANE STARR** - Age 18; a senior at the Academy; broad, built football star; good-looking and popular

*****PRINCE SHAWN STARR** - Age 18; a senior at the Academy; SHANE's twin; funny, friendly, but not as popular

PROFESSOR LEE WILSON - Approx. age 32; Speech teacher/homeroom monitor at the Academy; male; attractive and youthful

STUDENTS

FOOTBALL PLAYERS

CHEERLEADERS *(optional)*

SPECTATORS *(optional)*

*Note – **SHANE** and **SHAWN** may be played by the same actor if twins are not available.

TIME
The present; autumn

SETTING
A high school academy in Anytown, USA

THE SET

SET INSTRUCTIONS - This one-act consists of two different sets: a high-school classroom and a football field. Characters enter into the classroom from upstage right. Four rows of desks are spread across center stage facing the audience; each row contains three or four desks, depending on available space. The teacher's desk is located downstage left, facing the upstage right. For scenes occurring on the football field, clear the stage. A backdrop may be used to signify a field setting, if desired.

LIGHTING INSTRUCTIONS -
Scenes 1 and 3 – normal indoor lighting.
Scene 2 – outdoor daytime lighting
Scene 4 – outdoor night lighting; one spotlight needed

DON'T KISS THAT PRINCE!

CHARACTERS
(2M, 2W, 1 M/W; Extras)

(In order of appearance)

PRINCE ALAN ALARMING - Age 18; a senior at the Academy; athletic, good-looking, suave, and self-absorbed

PRINCE JONATHAN JOKESTER - Age 18; a senior at the Academy; average-looking, happy-go-lucky; a real class clown

PRINCESS MARIA MILD - Age 18; a senior at the Academy; nondescript, shy, intelligent, sweet; long-time crush on ALAN

PROFESSOR WHITE - Approx. age 55; biology teacher at the Academy; friendly, laid-back, understanding; may be male or female)

PRINCESS DESIREE DESIRE - Age 17; a junior at the Academy; good-looking, flirtatious, popular, and showy

STUDENTS - Ages 16-18

TIME
The present; spring

SETTING
A high school academy in Anytown, USA

THE SET

SET INSTRUCTIONS - This one-act consists of two different sets. The bulk of the action occurs in a science lab/classroom at the Academy. The entrance into the room is at stage right. The front of the classroom is stage left, where the professor's desk sits. Across upstage stands a black lab countertop with typical lab apparatus. The students' desks are arranged in rows at center stage, facing the teacher's desk at stage left. The other set is used only for Scene 2 and may take place outside the curtain, on a wing, or off to the side of stage right or left. This scene takes place in an old-fashioned ice cream parlor and consists merely of two white wrought iron-looking tables and four chairs. One of the tables with two chairs is placed in the center of the set and the other table and two chairs is off to stage right of the first table and set further upstage. The entrance into the parlor is stage right.

LIGHTING INSTRUCTIONS - For most of the play, the lighting is typical indoor lighting. Special attention should be given to the lighting instructions given in Scene 4. Three spotlights are needed for this play.

TWICE UPON A TIME

A One-Act Realistic Fantasy

SCENE ONE

SET: *A homeroom classroom at Anytown Academy; Monday morning*

(Students mill about the classroom, talking and laughing. Some are seated and hurriedly finishing homework. **AIDEN** *and* **LYNN** *are seated in the front rows of downstage left and talking, oblivious to a group of guys throwing a football back and forth right over their heads.* **CHRISTINA** *enters from upstage right,* **RENEE** *at her heels, and crosses to desks at downstage center. Both girls are dressed to attract attention. One of the football-throwing guys lets out a wolf whistle and* **CHRISTINA** *smiles flirtatiously.)*

CHRISTINA. Honestly, Renee. You would think they'd never seen princesses before! Anyway, back to the dress. I can't *wait* until you see it!

RENEE. It sounds totally gorgeous, Christina, but…how did you know you were going to be Homecoming Queen? I didn't even hear the nominees announced.

*(***CHRISTINA*** sets her purse down on the desk at downstage center.)*

CHRISTINA. *(Talking down to her)* Renee, Renee, Renee. You poor, sweet sophomore. It's a good thing I look out for you. The reason you haven't heard about the nominees is because they haven't been announced yet.

RENEE. Oh. But…you got a dress.

CHRISTINA. Yes, I did, and it is *so* beautiful!

RENEE. But how can you buy a dress when you don't even know if you're nominated?

CHRISTINA. Princess Renee! I'm surprised at you! You really don't know anything, do you?

*(Turns to **AIDEN**)*

Aiden, you've been at Anytown Academy since we were freshman. You should know. Renee doesn't understand why I already bought my Homecoming dress. Could you explain it to her?

(**CHRISTINA** *reaches into her purse and pulls out a compact.*)

LYNN. *(Rolling her eyes)* I can.

CHRISTINA. I didn't ask *you*, Lynn; I asked Aiden. Aiden, tell Renee why I bought my dress early. And why I *always* buy my dress early.

(**CHRISTINA** *proceeds to check her appearance in the mirror.*)

AIDEN. *(Rolling her eyes good-naturedly)* Are you at it again already, Christina? I keep telling you, being Homecoming Queen is not that big of a deal. We're all princesses already.

CHRISTINA. *(Snapping the compact shut)* You're only saying that because you've never been Homecoming Queen!

*(Turning to **RENEE**)*

I'll have you know that I have been elected the Homecoming Queen for the last two years.

(**LYNN** *imitates* **CHRISTINA***'s gestures and lip-synchs the statement dramatically behind* **CHRISTINA**. **AIDEN** *stifles a laugh, and* **CHRISTINA** *whirls around.*)

CHRISTINA *(Continued)* What? What's so funny?

LYNN. Nothing.

CHRISTINA. *(Eyes narrowing)* You'd better watch yourself, Lynn Leonardo. It would be a shame to be kicked off the cheerleading squad right before the big game.

LYNN. I'm not too concerned. Without me for a base, you'd never get off the ground.

(**CHRISTINA** *opens her mouth to respond, then pauses, confused. A second later, she turns to* **AIDEN**.)

CHRISTINA. Is she calling me fat?

(*Before* **RENEE** *can answer,* **PROFESSOR WILSON** *enters, carrying a briefcase and a cardboard box labeled "Homecoming Votes." He catches the football flying through the air as he walks by. The guys cheer.*)

PROFESSOR WILSON. All right, guys, that's enough. Have a seat.

(*The rest of the class begins taking their seats; there is still subdued chatter.*)

RENEE. (*Whispers to* **CHRISTINA**) Wow. Who is that?

CHRISTINA. *That* is Professor Wilson. He's our homeroom teacher. Isn't he hot?

RENEE. I wish my homeroom teacher looked like that! I've got old Professor Dinkleberry.

CHRISTINA. Poor thing.

(**PROFESSOR WILSON** *walks by* **RENEE** *and looks at her curiously.*)

PROFESSOR WILSON. Huh. Now what do we have here?

(*He sets his briefcase and the cardboard box on his desk at downstage left and picks up the roster on his desk.*)

PROFESSOR WILSON. (*Continued*) They didn't give me *another* student, did they?

(*To* **RENEE**)

Are you new?

RENEE. (*Breathlessly hopeful*) Yes?

PROFESSOR WILSON. (*With a suspicious grin*) What grade are you in?

RENEE. Tenth?

PROFESSOR WILSON. Sorry. You're in the wrong class. Better hurry.

(**RENEE** *stands up and picks up her purse, disappointedly.* **CHRISTINA** *flutters her fingers in a cheerful farewell.*)

CHRISTINA. See you later.

(**RENEE** *exits.*)

PROFESSOR WILSON. *(Amused)* Princess Christina, I think you'd better stop bringing your friends to homeroom. You're going to make them all tardy.

CHRISTINA. But I can't help it, Professor Wilson. They just seem to…follow me everywhere. It's just the penalty for being popular, I guess.

LYNN. Oh, brother.

PROFESSOR WILSON. *(Wryly)* Yes, well…speaking of popularity contests…I've got a couple announcements to make.

(*The* **PROFESSOR** *pulls a sheet of paper from his briefcase. The students quiet down in anticipation.*)

PROFESSOR WILSON. *(Continued)* I'm sure you're all aware that Friday night is the big Homecoming game against Elsewhere High. The game will be on the main field at seven o'clock sharp. During halftime, this year's Homecoming King and Queen will be crowned.

(*The students cheer and whistle.* **PROFESSOR WILSON** *gestures for them to quiet down.*)

PROFESSOR WILSON. *(Continued. Good-naturedly)* Okay, okay. Save it for the game.

(*The class quiets.*)

Thank you.

(*With mock drama*)

And now, it is my honor and privilege to announce to you your Homecoming nominees…

(*The school bell rings.* **CHRISTINA** *sits up straight in her chair, folds her hands, and smiles knowingly. The rest of the students listen attentively.* **PROFESSOR WILSON** *unfolds a sheet of paper.)*

PROFESSOR WILSON. *(Continued)* For Homecoming King, the nominees for this year are –

(The classroom door upstage right suddenly opens with a bang. The class starts and turns to stare as **SHANE STARR** *saunters into the classroom.* **SHANE** *wears a football jersey and his hair is messy in a roguish, attractive way. He walks along the last aisle of desks, stage right, moving to his seat at downstage right.)*

PROFESSOR WILSON. *(Continued)* Prince Shane. So nice of you to join us.

SHANE. Hey, no problem.

(He flashes a grin at the **PROFESSOR** *and a wink at a few girls as he moves to his desk. The girls giggle and blush.* **CHRISTINA** *raises her eyebrows and shows signs of interest in* **SHANE.***)*

PROFESSOR WILSON. I wonder if Coach O'Malley would have the same response if you showed up late to football practice as often as you show up late to class.

SHANE. *(With a laid-back grin)* Hey, man, chill out. I'm, like, a whole five seconds late. Besides, it's just homeroom.

(He tosses his notebook on his desk and sits, leaning back in his seat, stretching his legs out in front of him and folding his arms behind his head. He glances over at **CHRISTINA** *on his left.)*

SHANE *(Continued)* Hey, beautiful…did I miss anything?

PROFESSOR WILSON. *(Under his breath)* Besides the point? No.

*(***CHRISTINA** *smiles flirtatiously but says nothing.* **SHANE** *smiles back appreciatively.)*

PROFESSOR WILSON. *(Continued)* As I was saying, the nominees for Homecoming King this year are as follows: Prince Joshua Janasak…

BOY IN BACK ROW. Yeah, Janasak!

(A few guys hoot.)

PROFESSOR WILSON. . . . .Prince Michael Miller, and…

(Conceding)

Prince Shane Starr.

*(**SHANE** grins and nods knowingly while most of the room–the girls in particular–burst into whistles and applause.)*

PROFESSOR WILSON. *(Continued. Wryly)* Well, Shane, I guess it's a good thing they don't disqualify people for tardiness.

*(The class chuckles and **SHANE** crosses his arms across his chest with a self-satisfied smile.)*

Now for Homecoming Queen…

(The class quiets down again. The girls in the classroom perk up.)

This year's nominees are… Princess Jessica Jordan, Princess Christina Carlyle, and Princess Aiden Alexander.

*(Both **AIDEN** and **CHRISTINA** respond in shock upon hearing **AIDEN**'s name. **LYNN** turns to **AIDEN** excitedly.)*

LYNN. Aiden, you're in!

AIDEN. I can't believe it!

CHRISTINA. Neither can I!

*(To **PROFESSOR WILSON**)*

Professor Wilson, are you sure that list is accurate?

PROFESSOR WILSON. I'm pretty sure it is, Christina. Why? Is there a problem?

CHRISTINA. Yes. There can't be *two* of us from the cheerleading squad running for Homecoming Queen!

LYNN. Why not?

PROFESSOR WILSON. Yes, why not?

CHRISTINA. *(Sputtering)* Well…because…because it's never happened that way, that's all! I have *never* had to run against one of my own cheerleaders. I'm the captain.

It's just...wrong!

PROFESSOR WILSON. Well, Princess Christina...despite the way you may feel, I don't believe there's any rule against it. Homecoming nominees are strictly by vote.

(**CHRISTINA** *sits back and lets out an indignant huff of disbelief.*)

PROFESSOR WILSON. *(Continued. Looking back down at the sheet)* Which leads me to the next announcement.... Each student will be allowed one vote for Homecoming King and one vote for Homecoming Queen. All votes must be cast by Thursday morning and may be cast only in your homeroom's voting box. The winners will be announced Friday morning during homeroom.

SHANE. Guess that means I'll have to be on time Friday, huh?

PROFESSOR WILSON. *(Good-naturedly)* Yes, well, we all have to make sacrifices, Shane.

SHANE. Anybody got an extra alarm clock?

(*The school bell rings. The students start to gather their things and stand.*)

PROFESSOR WILSON. *(To the class)* Well, that's it for announcements. Have a good day!

(*To* **SHANE**)

Shane, could I speak to you for a moment?

(*The students begin to exit upstage right and* **SHANE** *sheepishly crosses to* **PROFESSOR WILSON**, *who walks him over to upstage right and talks to him quietly. At downstage left,* **LYNN** *turns to* **AIDEN** *and gives her a hug.* **CHRISTINA** *hangs back, watching them coolly.*)

LYNN. Congratulations, Aiden! I am so excited for you! I just know you're going to win!

AIDEN. Thanks, Lynn.

CHRISTINA. Awwww...How sweet. *(Businesslike)* Aiden, we'll talk at cheerleading practice. Don't be late.

(**CHRISTINA** *eyes* **LYNN** *coolly for a moment and then* *exits.* **AIDEN***'s smile fades.)*

LYNN. *(Rolling her eyes)* Don't worry about her, Aiden. There's nothing she can do and she knows it. You and I'll put on the best campaign this school has ever seen.

AIDEN. Lynn, I...I really don't want to campaign. I'm just not comfortable with this whole thing. It's not worth it.

LYNN. Not worth it? A chance to show up Little-Miss Dictator-of-the-World? Of course it is! Look, I'll see you at lunch. We'll talk then, okay?

AIDEN. Yeah...okay.

LYNN. See you later.

AIDEN. *(Somewhat distracted)* Bye.

*(**LYNN** exits, **AIDEN**'s gaze lingering on the voting box. She takes a few indecisive steps toward the voting box. **PROFESSOR WILSON** finishes speaking to **SHANE** and exits as **LYNN** does. **SHANE** returns to his seat quickly to grab his pen. The other students have already exited and the room is empty except for **SHANE** and **AIDEN**. **SHANE** glances over at **AIDEN**.)*

SHANE. *(In a softer voice than previously)* Hey. You're Princess Aiden, aren't you?

*(**AIDEN** looks up, surprised to find someone else still in the room. Then she smiles.)*

AIDEN. *(Gently reproving)* Shane! We've been in the same homeroom for the last two months and you're only just *now* figuring that out? Maybe you *should* come to class on time more often.

*(**AIDEN** shakes her head with a smile, picks up her books, and makes a move to exit upstage right.)*

SHANE. Actually, I kind of have a confession to make.

AIDEN. Let me guess. You really belong in the homeroom for Over-sleepers Anonymous?

SHAWN. *(With a grin)* No, *I* don't. But my brother sure does. I'm Shawn, Shane's twin brother.

*(**SHAWN** holds out his hand and **AIDEN** shakes it in-*

credulously.)

AIDEN. That's right! I heard Shane had a twin brother. You're the actor, aren't you?

SHAWN. *(Dramatically)* The lady has found me out.

AIDEN. Wow. Well, you certainly did an amazing job imitating Shane today. That was just like him.

SHAWN. Well, I've had plenty of time to study the role.

AIDEN. So where is he anyway?

SHAWN. Oversleeping, as usual.

(Glancing at his watch)

Actually, he's probably just getting up.

AIDEN. Won't you get in trouble for missing *your* homeroom?

SHAWN. Probably. But not as much trouble as Shane would get in. The office told him if he's late to one more class they aren't going to let him play in the game on Friday.

AIDEN. Yikes! That would *not* be good. He's our star quarterback!

SHAWN. Yeah, I know. He never lets me forget it!

(SHAWN glances down at his watch.)

SHAWN. *(Continued)* Well, it's about time for Shane to be in Remedial Math class, so I guess it's big brother to the rescue again.

AIDEN. Good thing you're a professional.

SHAWN. *(With a half-bow)* Thank you for the compliment. It's been a pleasure meeting you, Aiden. And congratulations on the nomination. You really do deserve it, you know. I hope you win.

AIDEN. Thank you. It was good to meet you, too.

(SHAWN starts to leave, then stops.)

SHAWN. *(Hesitantly)* Hey, I don't suppose you'd be interested in a free ticket to *The Importance of Being Earnest*? We're putting on a special pre-game matinee Friday. It's kind of like a by-invitation-only dress rehearsal. If you're busy with cheerleading duties, I understand. It *is* Homecoming night after all, and I'm sure you –

AIDEN. No! I'd love to come, Shane...I mean, Shawn. Sorry.

SHAWN. *(With a wink)* That's all right. Happens all the time.

*(**SHAWN** pulls a ticket out of his pocket and hands it to **AIDEN**.)*

AIDEN. Thank you. And what character are you in the play? Ernest?

SHAWN. *(Laughing)* Isn't everyone? See you Friday.

AIDEN. Bye, Shawn.

*(**AIDEN** looks down at the ticket as **SHAWN** exits upstage right. She looks up when she hears the door shut and over at the voting box thoughtfully.)*

AIDEN. *(Continued)* Maybe he's right. Maybe I do deserve it.

*(With a sudden look of determination, **AIDEN** grabs a slip of paper and writes down her name in big letters.)*

AIDEN. *(Continued. Announcing)* Princess Aiden Alexander, Homecoming Queen.

(After a thoughtful pause, she smiles.)

Why not?

*(**AIDEN** drops the slip in the box. Lights fade.)*

End of Scene.

SCENE TWO

SET: *Anytown football field, an empty stage except for a bench placed at center; that afternoon*

SOUND: *A coach's whistle blows and football practice sound effects may be used as background noise.*

(**AIDEN** *and* **LYNN** *enter from stage right, their arms linked and heads together as if sharing a secret. They are dressed for cheerleading practice except for their flip-flops. They are carrying their tennis shoes. A* **FOOTBALL PLAYER** *in practice gear enters stage left sprinting across the stage, breathing hard. He accidentally bumps into* **LYNN**.)

FOOTBALL PLAYER. Oh. Sorry, Lynn.

LYNN. That's okay, Sam.

(*The* **FOOTBALL PLAYER** *exits stage right as* **AIDEN** *and* **LYNN** *reach center.*)

LYNN. *(Continued)* So he gave you a ticket to the matinee? Aiden, that is so sweet! I still can't believe that wasn't Shane! I mean, talk about a perfect imitation.

AIDEN. I know! Wasn't it amazing?

LYNN. He must be one good actor! You are going to his play, aren't you?

AIDEN. I really want to, but what about Christina? You know she'll have us working our tails off getting everything set up and decorated for Homecoming.

LYNN. Please. I'll handle Christina. *You* go to that dress rehearsal. This Shawn guy sounds sweet, and who knows? You two may turn out to be more than just friends. And I'm not going to let you pass up that opportunity!

AIDEN. Lynn…you're the best.

LYNN. I know.

(**CHRISTINA** *enters stage left, a red whistle hanging around her neck. She is dressed in red shorts and a white*

T-shirt and is wearing white tennis shoes and an expensive wrist watch.)

CHRISTINA. Girls! It is now 3:38! Practice starts at 3:45 and you're haven't even put on your cheerleading shoes yet!

LYNN. *(To* **AIDEN***)* Wow! It's only 3:38? That means we've got seven more minutes to talk!

(To **CHRISTINA***)*

Thanks, Christina! I don't know what we'd do without your Rolex.

CHRISTINA. Must I remind you of the penalty for being late to practice?

LYNN. Yeah, yeah, we know. Twenty laps around the track.

CHRISTINA. Well…??

LYNN. Christina, have we ever been late before?

CHRISTINA. Well…no.

LYNN. Okay then. See you in seven minutes.

CHRISTINA. Six minutes.

(Disgusted, **CHRISTINA** *whirls around and stomps off stage left.)*

AIDEN. You're really good at getting on her last nerve, aren't you?

LYNN. I like to think of it as an art.

AIDEN. Lynn, it's funny and all, but don't get in trouble over it. If you don't get to cheer in the game on Friday…

LYNN. Me? Not cheer? Please. Ain't never gonna happen! I told you. She needs me for a base. I'm the only one that can lift her!

*(***LYNN** *sits down on the bench at center.* **AIDEN** *follows her lead. They both begin putting on their tennis shoes.)*

LYNN. *(Continued)* Now forget about Christina for a few minutes and let's focus on Aiden. We've still got to plan this whole Homecoming shebang, because I know you're going to win. And I'm going to help you figure out everything from the dress to the smooch.

AIDEN. *(Alarmed)* Smooch? Lynn, what are you talking about?

LYNN. You know. The big "Play Ball!" smooch between the new Homecoming King and Queen.

AIDEN. They have to kiss??

LYNN. Well, yeah. But it's no big deal, Aiden. It's just a tradition. It doesn't really mean anything.

AIDEN. But, Lynn! I've never kissed a guy in my entire life!

LYNN. I know that. That's why I said I'm going to help you. Everything from the dress to the smooch, remember?

AIDEN. You don't understand!

LYNN. Sure I do. Heck, I've been kissing guys since…I don't know…maybe fourth grade…

AIDEN. No, that's not what I mean! Lynn, I *can't* kiss any guys. Not yet anyway.

LYNN. Why not? Are you…waiting until you get married or something?

AIDEN. *(Quietly)* Something like that.

LYNN. *(Becoming serious)* Aiden, it's all right. You can tell me. Did…something happen?

AIDEN. *(With a sigh)* Yes. But…but not with me.

LYNN. You're right; I don't understand.

AIDEN. Lynn, we don't have enough time to –

LYNN. Yes, we do. You've got four minutes. Spill.

AIDEN. Okay, then. Short version. You know how my mom died a few minutes after I was born?

LYNN. Right. I knew that.

AIDEN. Well, here's the problem. Before that happened, there had been this weird nurse at that hospital – at least, Dad *thought* she was a nurse – and for some reason, she had a huge crush on my dad. She wrote him all these love letters even while my mom was in the hospital. Anyway, she told him that he was going to have a little girl and that he had to name her Agatha.

That was *her* name.

LYNN. Ew!

AIDEN. Tell me about it! She said that if he *didn't* name me Agatha, something bad would happen. So my dad decided that he wasn't going to risk it. He was going to name me Agatha. And then my mom died, and…and he just couldn't go through with it. He gave me the name Aiden. My mother's name.

LYNN. And it's a beautiful name.

AIDEN. Well, Agatha didn't think so. She was furious! She stormed into the hospital room and she…

LYNN. *(Leaning in with interest)* What? She what?

AIDEN. She…put a curse on me.

LYNN. *(Skeptical)* A curse? You mean like voodoo or something?

AIDEN. Yes. She said that if I kissed anyone who wasn't "The One," I'd send him into a hundred-year coma.

LYNN. "The One"? What is that supposed to mean?

AIDEN. You know, "The One." My one true love.

LYNN. Oh, good grief. What kind of psychopaths do they have working at these hospitals anyway? Aiden, don't you believe her for a minute! There is no possible way you could ever put anyone into a hundred-year coma.

AIDEN. But it's true! Do you remember Prince Ryan?

LYNN. Ryan Romano? Yeah, I remember him. He's the one who moved to Nowhere, right?

AIDEN. Wrong! He still lives in Anytown. Right over on Hillcrest. He's in a coma, Lynn!

(Quietly)

For at least another ninety-eight years.

LYNN. Aiden! I thought you told me you never kissed anyone!

AIDEN. I didn't! He kissed me! I didn't even have a chance to stop him.

LYNN. Wow. Ryan's in a coma? How come none of us ever heard about it?

AIDEN. My dad worked it out with his parents somehow. It's supposed to be top secret. If anyone ever found out, I could be...

LYNN. Don't worry, Aiden. I'm not going to tell anybody.

AIDEN. Thank you.

(CHRISTINA enters quietly from upstage left. AIDEN and LYNN don't notice her arrival. When she begins to speak, they jump in surprise.)

LYNN. Wow, but what are we going to do about this kiss?

AIDEN. I don't know.

CHRISTINA. Oh, what's wrong, Aiden? Afraid of a little smooch? Guess you'll just have to leave the title of Homecoming Queen to me. After all, I'm the more experienced.

LYNN. *(Under her breath)* I'll say.

CHRISTINA. Shut your mouth, Lynn Leonardo. I know what you're trying to say. *(To AIDEN; condescendingly)* Aiden, dear, you really have nothing to worry about. You haven't got a shot at that title anyway, you know. That crown's got "Christina Carlyle" written all over it. Just like every year.

(LYNN stands.)

LYNN. Christina, why don't you just –

AIDEN. Well, maybe not this year.

LYNN & CHRISTINA. *(Both turning to look at AIDEN)* What?

AIDEN. I said, maybe not this year.

LYNN. You mean you're still going for it?

CHRISTINA. You can't do that! Aiden, as your cheerleading captain, I *order* you to drop out of the race for Homecoming Queen!

AIDEN. No.

CHRISTINA. No?!

AIDEN. No. Christina, if you deserve the title as much as you think you do, then you've got nothing to worry about. You'll win again like usual. But I'm still going to try for it.

*(**AIDEN** stands and moves toward stage left exit. **LYNN** follows suit. **CHRISTINA** stares at her aghast.)*

CHRISTINA. But…you can't!…Aiden Alexander!

*(**AIDEN** stops and looks at her watch.)*

AIDEN. By the way, Christina, it's now 3:47. You're late. I guess we'll see you on the track after practice.

*(**CHRISTINA** glances down at her watch and stifles a scream of frustration as she storms past **AIDEN** and **LYNN** and off stage left. **AIDEN** and **LYNN** look at one another and smile.)*

LYNN. Well. I have only one thing to say to that. You go, your Majesty!

*(**AIDEN** and **LYNN** high five and exit stage left as lights fade.)*

End of Scene.

SCENE THREE

SET: **PROFESSOR WILSON**'s *homeroom classroom at Anytown Academy; Friday morning*

(The scene is very similar to Scene 1. Students mill about the classroom, talking and laughing. Some are seated and hurriedly finishing homework. The general atmosphere, however, is more excited and anticipatory. **SHANE** *is seated at downstage right talking to several girls on his left from the class.* **AIDEN** *and* **LYNN** *are also in their seats in the front rows at stage left. As lights rise,* **CHRISTINA** *enters the classroom from upstage right. As she makes her way downstage, she stops at each desk, smiles playfully, and hands its occupant a lollipop. The lollipops have little flags on them that say "Christina Carlyle for Homecoming Queen.")*

CHRISTINA. *(To* **BOY IN BACK***)* Hi! Who did you vote for for Homecoming Queen?...Really? Well, thank you!

(She places a lollipop on his desk and moves on.)

CHRISTINA. *(Continued)* How about you? Did you vote for me for Homecoming Queen?

AIDEN. *(Turning around to stare at* **CHRISTINA***)* What is she doing?

CHRISTINA. Thank you! You're so sweet.

LYNN. *(Wryly)* The same thing she's been doing all week.

AIDEN. Isn't bribery illegal?

LYNN. I think it's more like reimbursement. The actual bribery ended yesterday when voting closed.

CHRISTINA. *(To* **GIRL IN MIDDLE***)* Hi! So who did you vote for?

(She pauses, hands on hips, and waits for the answer. She then makes a face and grabs the lollipop.)

CHRISTINA. *(Continued)* Give me that!

LYNN. Looks like she's only been somewhat successful with it anyways. I wouldn't worry about her, Aiden.

AIDEN. I'm not.

(**AIDEN** *returns to fidgeting with her pens and pencils.*)

LYNN. Are you nervous? Today's the big day.

AIDEN. I know.

LYNN. Don't worry. You're going to win. I've had, like, five dozen people tell me they voted for you.

AIDEN. That's what I'm worried about! What if I *do* win? What am I going to do about the kiss?

LYNN. Hmm…that is a big one. Maybe you could fake it.

AIDEN. How am I supposed to do that?

LYNN. I don't know. It was just an idea.

(**CHRISTINA** *has reached* **SHANE**'s *desk by this time. The girls who had been talking to* **SHANE** *move back to their seats once* **CHRISTINA** *approaches.*)

SHANE. *(To* **CHRISTINA***)* Hey, beautiful. Passing out sweets?

(**SHANE** *reaches up and pulls* **CHRISTINA** *into his lap.*)

SHANE. *(Continued)* I'll take this one.

CHRISTINA. *(Laughing coyly)* Prince Shane! Or should I call you King Shane? I'm sure *you're* going to win.

SHANE. You're too kind.

CHRISTINA. Wouldn't you want me for your Homecoming Queen?

(**PROFESSOR WILSON** *enters from upstage right in time to hear* **SHANE**'s *response and walks downstage using center aisle.*)

SHANE. I don't know. Depends on how well you can kiss.

CHRISTINA. Would you like to find out?

PROFESSOR WILSON. No, I don't think so. Shane, Christina, why don't you two wait until science class to perform any of those kinds of experiments. I'd hate for something to blow up in my homeroom.

CHRISTINA. If you say so, Professor.

(**CHRISTINA** *slides off* **SHANE**'s *lap and sits in the desk stage left of his. The school bells rings.*)

PROFESSOR WILSON. All right, let's get started. Since I know this is what you've all been waiting for…

(**PROFESSOR WILSON** *pulls a sheet of paper out of his briefcase and holds it up.*)

PROFESSOR WILSON *(Continued)* The results of the Homecoming King and Queen elections!

(The students applaud and whistle eagerly.)

Thank you, thank you. I take cash, check, and credit card.

(Clearing his throat)

And now…the moment you've all been waiting for…

(The students quiet down.)

PROFESSOR WILSON *(cont'd)* The title of Homecoming King this year goes to… Prince Shane Starr!

(Wild applause, whistles, and cheers. **SHANE** *jumps up, raises his arms in victory, and whoops.)*

SHANE. Yeah! All right! Who's the king?

PROFESSOR WILSON. I think that's the most excited I've ever seen you off the football field, Shane.

(Grinning, **SHANE** *moves back toward his seat.)*

SHANE. So where's my crown?

PROFESSOR WILSON. You'll get it tonight.

SHANE. *(Sitting down)* Yeah, baby!

PROFESSOR WILSON. *(Shaking his head and chuckling under his breath)* And now for the title of Homecoming Queen…

(The room quiets. **CHRISTINA** *leans forward slightly.* **AIDEN** *nervously glances at* **LYNN**, *who smiles excitedly.)*

PROFESSOR WILSON. *(Continued)* This year's race for Homecoming Queen was very close. In fact, it came down to a difference of only fourteen votes. But…this year's Homecoming Queen is…Princess Aiden Alexander!

(The students applaud and cheer. **AIDEN**'s *mouth falls open in surprise.)*

CHRISTINA. What?!

(**LYNN** *cheers and throws her arms around* **AIDEN**.)

LYNN. Aiden! You did it! You beat Christina! You're the Homecoming Queen!

AIDEN. I can't believe it!

(**CHRISTINA** *jumps to her feet.*)

CHRISTINA. *(To* **PROFESSOR WILSON***)* There's got to be some mistake!

PROFESSOR WILSON. Not again, Christina.

CHRISTINA. I demand a recount!

(**CHRISTINA** *crosses to* **PROFESSOR WILSON**. *They begin to argue silently,* **CHRISTINA** *gesturing expressively.*)

AIDEN. *(Pulling back from their hug)* But, Lynn, what I'm going to do about –

LYNN. Don't worry about that now! You won! Enjoy the moment!

(**LYNN** *hugs* **AIDEN** *again.* **SHANE** *crosses to* **AIDEN**.)

SHANE. Hey, Princess! Congratulations. Not who I thought would win, but I'm okay with that.

AIDEN. Uh, thanks, Shane.

CHRISTINA. Isn't someone going to do something about the injustice here?!

SHANE. *(To* **AIDEN***)* Hey, I got an idea.

(**SHANE** *pulls* **AIDEN** *to her feet.*)

Professor Wilson, I know you said no science experiments in homeroom, but I think it'd be a good idea if Aiden and I practiced for the big smacks tonight.

(To **AIDEN***)*

What do say, Aiden? How about a little kiss for your king?

(**SHANE** *leans in and puckers up.* **LYNN** *and* **CHRISTINA** *watch aghast.*)

AIDEN. Shane! Don't!!!

(**AIDEN** *dodges his lips and he lands a kiss in mid-air, nearly falling over. The students laugh.* **CHRISTINA** *smiles smugly.*)

BOY IN THE BACK. Nice one, Shane. Real smooth.

SHANE. *(To* **AIDEN***)* Hey! What gives?

CHRISTINA. Oh, sorry, Shane. I should have warned you. Aiden doesn't kiss boys. She doesn't know how.

SHANE. *(Looking at* **AIDEN***)* Are you serious?

(**AIDEN** *rolls her eyes.*)

CHRISTINA. So you see, Professor Wilson, we do have a legitimate problem here. How can you have a Homecoming Queen that refuses to kiss the Homecoming King?

PROFESSOR WILSON. Princess Christina, I'm sorry but the vote is final. I'm sure Aiden will do just fine tonight.

(**SHANE** *drapes an arm across* **AIDEN***'s shoulder.*)

SHANE. *(Lowering his voice)* Hey, babe, if you want to come over this afternoon, I can give you a couple lessons before the –

(**AIDEN** *shakes off his hand.*)

AIDEN. Let go of me!

(**AIDEN** *moves toward upstage right exit.*)

SHANE. *(To* **AIDEN***; trying to laugh it off)* Hey! You know, we're gonna have problems if this happens tonight, you realize…Aiden?

(**LYNN** *jumps up and follows* **AIDEN** *out. The door slams behind them. There is a brief pause.*)

PROFESSOR WILSON. So…Prince Shane…Are you always this charming with the ladies?

SHANE. *(Good-naturedly)* Well, you know…most of them like it.

(**SHANE** *wraps his arm around* **CHRISTINA***'s shoulders. She lets out a disgusted huff, brushes his arm off, and storms out upstage right. The class watches her leave.*)

SHANE. *(Continued)* What I do?

(SHANE throws up his arms and drops into a seat. The school bell rings. Lights fade.)

End of Scene.

SCENE FOUR

SET: *Anytown football field, an empty stage; Homecoming night.*

LIGHTING: *Stage lights should be set dimmer than previous scenes.*

(As **AIDEN** *and* **SHAWN** *enter stage right and stop downstage right, a spotlight rises on them.* **AIDEN** *is wearing her Homecoming dress and her hair is styled up.* **SHAWN** *is wearing dark dress pants and a white collar shirt.)*

AIDEN. Shawn, you were amazing!

SHAWN. So you liked it? The play, I mean.

AIDEN. Shawn, it was fabulous! I can't believe it was only a dress rehearsal. You looked like a professional up there!

SHAWN. Well, maybe someday. But I'm glad you liked it.

AIDEN. Thank you so much for inviting me.

SHAWN. Hey, no problem. Maybe…maybe we could get together again sometime. Preferably some place where I don't have to watch you from a distance.

AIDEN. I'd like that.

SHAWN. How about after the game?

AIDEN. Wow! You work fast!

SHAWN. Have to. I'm trying to get a date with the Homecoming Queen.

AIDEN. *(Teasing)* You sure you're not just asking me out *because* I'm the Homecoming Queen?

*(***SHAWN** *reaches out for* **AIDEN***'s hand and pulls her toward him.)*

SHAWN. No. I'm asking you out because you're Princess Aiden. And because I think you're a very special person.

(They gaze into one another's eyes for a moment. **SHAWN** *leans in.* **AIDEN** *closes her eyes, and* **SHAWN** *gives her a soft, brief kiss on the lips. He pulls back and smiles.* **AIDEN** *opens her eyes, still in a dreamy daze.)*

SHAWN. *(Continued)* I'll see you after the game.

(**SHAWN** *crosses stage and exits stage left.* **AIDEN** *watches him leave dreamily. Then, her eyes widen and she starts in realization. Her hand flies to her mouth.*)

AIDEN. Oh no! What have I done?

(**LYNN**, *in cheerleading uniform, enters stage right.*)

LYNN. Aiden?

AIDEN. Lynn! Lynn, what am I going to do?!

LYNN. Hey, it's okay, honey, just calm down.

AIDEN. But you don't understand! I just –

LYNN. Whoa! Relax, Aiden! I've got the kiss all figured out.

AIDEN. You do?

LYNN. Yep. All you have to do is turn your head just like you did in class today, and you'll be fine. Just try to do it without making Shane look like an idiot. Even though both you and I know he is.

AIDEN. What if he's ready for it and I can't avoid him?

LYNN. Well, I figure with the way that boy oversleeps, it would take a few weeks for anyone to even realize something was wrong with him.

AIDEN. *(With a hesitant smile)* You really think I can do this?

LYNN. Aiden, I know you can. Now, I'm going to go get a good spot on the bleachers. If you get nervous, just look for me. I'll be cheering for you the entire time.

AIDEN. Thanks, Lynn. I don't know what I'd do without you.

(**PROFESSOR WILSON**, *dressed in a suit and tie, enters from upstage left carrying a microphone and stand and walks toward center. He sets the microphone stand down just left of center stage and speaks into the microphone, looking out over the audience.*)

PROFESSOR WILSON. All right. If I could have your attention please, we'll get things started.

LYNN. See you after the ceremony.

(**LYNN** *gives* **AIDEN**'s *arm one last squeeze and exits downstage right to take a seat in the actual audience. As she exits,* **SHANE** *enters, stage left, and crosses to* **AIDEN** *at stage right. He is dressed in a black tux. While* **SHANE** *and* **AIDEN** *speak to one another, the football team enters upstage and lines up across upstage. They are in uniform and look raring to go.*)

SHANE. Hey there, beautiful! Looks like I'm just in time.

AIDEN. I don't suppose you know the meaning of the word "early"?

SHANE. Nah. Life's more fun when you live on the edge. You should try it sometime.

(**SHANE** *hands her a red rose.*)

Here you go. I got you something.

(**AIDEN** *looks back at him. With a look of surprise, she slowly accepts the rose.*)

AIDEN. What's this for?

SHANE. A pretty flower for a pretty girl.

(**AIDEN** *looks away with a smile.*)

PROFESSOR WILSON. Okay. It looks like we're ready to begin.

(*The crowd quiets.*)

Good evening. My name is Professor Lee Wilson, and it is my privilege to welcome you here tonight to Anytown Academy's Homecoming game against the Elsewhere Eagles.

(*Cheers and applause. May be from performers placed in audience, behind audience, backstage, or canned.*)

But first, as it is our tradition here at Anytown Academy, I'd like to introduce to you this year's Homecoming King and Queen.

(*Cheers and applause.* **PROFESSOR WILSON** *motions for* **SHANE** *and* **AIDEN** *to join him center stage. A pouty* **CHRISTINA** *in cheerleading uniform and a* **FOOTBALL**

PLAYER *enter stage left, each carrying a red velvet pillow with a crown on it.)*

PROFESSOR WILSON. *(Continued)* Allow me to present this year's Homecoming King – Prince Shane Starr.

(Cheers and applause. **SHANE** *raises a hand in greeting as he looks out over the audience.* **PROFESSOR WILSON** *takes the crown from the* **FOOTBALL PLAYER**, *removes* **SHANE***'s usual crown, and places the Homecoming crown on* **SHANE***'s head.* **SHANE** *bends over the microphone to speak into it.)*

SHANE. *(To* **PROFESSOR WILSON***)* Thanks, man. *(To audience)* Well, first of all, I'd like to thank my mom –

PROFESSOR WILSON. Shane. You don't have to make a speech.

SHANE. Really? All right then.

*(***SHANE** *steps back with a grin. Cheers and applause.* **FOOTBALL PLAYER** *joins his teammates upstage.)*

PROFESSOR WILSON. And now, allow me to present to you your Homecoming Queen – Princess Aiden Alexander.

(Cheers and applause even louder than before. **AIDEN** *steps forward with a tentative smile.* **CHRISTINA** *narrows her eyes.* **PROFESSOR WILSON** *has to call* **CHRISTINA***'s name to get her attention. Unwillingly, she thrusts the pillow toward* **PROFESSOR WILSON**, *who takes the crown, removes* **AIDEN***'s usual crown, and places the Homecoming crown on* **AIDEN***'s head.* **AIDEN** *waves at the audience tentatively.)*

PROFESSOR WILSON. *(Continued)* Now if I could have our Homecoming King join me in the center here.

*(***SHANE** *moves back to center beside* **PROF. WILSON**. **CHRISTINA** *backs up to the edge of stage left, arms crossed.)*

PROFESSOR WILSON. *(Continued)* As most of you know, we here at Anytown Academy have a little Homecoming tradition –

(**PROF. WILSON** *is interrupted by the* **FOOTBALL PLAYERS**' *hoots and whistles.*)

PROFESSOR WILSON. *(Continued. To* **PLAYERS***)* All right, guys, that's enough. *(To audience)* As you can see, they always look forward to it. And that is the traditional kiss between our new Homecoming King and Queen.

(*Cheers and applause.* **AIDEN** *looks down with a nervous smile.* **SHANE** *looks out at audience, nodding his head and grinning. He raises his arms to encourage the audience to cheer louder.* **CHRISTINA** *smiles smugly.*)

PROFESSOR WILSON. *(Continued)* And so for one last time I give you Prince Shane Starr and Princess Aiden Alexander, your Homecoming King and Queen.

(**PROFESSOR WILSON** *motions toward the couple. Cheers and applause.* **SHANE** *turns toward* **AIDEN**, *their eyes locking.*)

SHANE. You know…I've always wanted to do a scene with a kiss.

(**AIDEN** *freezes.*)

But only if it was with the right girl.

AIDEN. *(Whisper)* Shawn??

SHAWN. *(In low voice)* Shh. You'll give me away.

(**SHAWN** *leans in and kisses her on the lips. Cheers and applause.*)

PROFESSOR WILSON. *(To audience)* Well, if this ceremony is any indication, it looks like it's going to be a dynamite night for the Anytown Angels! So let's get this game started!

(*Cheers and applause.* **SHAWN** *pulls back and grins at* **AIDEN**. **PROFESSOR WILSON** *picks up microphone and stand and exits stage left.* **CHRISTINA** *stomps off after him. The* **FOOTBALL PLAYERS** *jog off upstage left jumping around, cheering, and smacking one another* *excitedly.)*

AIDEN. Shawn! You're awake! I mean...you're okay!

SHAWN. Better than okay!

AIDEN. But...where's Shane?

SHAWN. You mean Sleeping Beauty? In the locker room. But don't worry about him. He owes me one.

(SHAWN locks arms with AIDEN as they move downstage left.)

SHAWN. *(Continued)* You see, once upon a time I saved his neck from being late to homeroom.

AIDEN. *(Slowly; with realization)* You mean twice upon a time, don't you?

SHAWN. The lady has found me out. Again.

AIDEN. Don't feel too bad. You're still good enough to be a professional.

SHAWN. Maybe. But after tonight, I think I'll just be me for awhile. Because I must say, it is certainly much more enjoyable when you're *not* running away from me!

(SHAWN and AIDEN kiss. Cheers and applause. Lights fade.)

End of Scene.

END OF PLAY

APPENDIX

Prop List

Books, notebooks, pencils, pens, paper, etc: for the students

Nerf football: for football-throwing students

Purse with compact mirror: for Christina

Briefcase with roster, nominees list, and winners list: for Professor Wilson

Cardboard box labeled "Homecoming Votes": for Professor Wilson

Dress rehearsal ticket: for Shawn

White tennis shoes: for Aiden and Lynn

Whistle: for Christina

Bag of lollipops with flags reading "Christina Carlyle for Homecoming Queen": for Christina

Microphone and stand: for Professor Wilson

Red rose: for Shane

Two red velvet pillows with Homecoming King and Queen crowns: for Christina and Football Player

Costume List

Note: This play is a modern-day twist on a fairy tale myth. Therefore, although the costumes are contemporary, each student wears a crown at all times. The crowns should fit each character's personality. The teacher, however, dresses in traditional royal garb. Some suggestions for student dress and Professor Wilson's dress are given below:

Princess Christina Carlyle –

<u>Scenes 1 & 3</u>: An outfit to attract attention; high heels; jewel-studded crown; meticulously applied makeup; fake nails

<u>Scene 2</u>: Red shorts, white T-shirt, tennis shoes, and an expensive watch

<u>Scene 4</u>: Red and white cheerleading outfit; white tennis shoes; red face paint on one cheek that says "Go Team" or something to that effect

Princess Renee Richards –

An outfit to attract attention; high heels *(but not as high as Christina's)*; smaller jewel-studded crown; a miniature version of Christina

Princess Lynn Leonardo –

<u>Scenes 1 & 3</u>: Jeans and a nice shirt *(casual but tasteful)*; simple crown

<u>Scene 2</u>: Exercise clothes and flip-flops *(carrying tennis shoes)*

<u>Scene 4</u>: Red and white cheerleading outfit; white tennis shoes; red face paint on one cheek that says "Go Team" or something to that effect

Princess Aiden Alexander –

<u>Scenes 1 & 3</u>: The middle ground between Christina and Lynn; maybe a stylish skirt-and- shirt combo; small crown with a few gems on it

<u>Scene 2</u>: Exercise clothes and flip-flops *(carrying tennis shoes)*

<u>Scene 4</u>: A knee-length formal dress; high heels; an updo hairstyle

Prince Shane/Shawn Starr –

<u>Scenes 1 & 3</u>: Jeans and a football jersey; basic gold crown

<u>Scene 4</u>: As Shawn: Black dress pants and a white, button-down collar shirt, dress shoes

As Shane: Add tuxedo jacket and bowtie to Shawn's attire

Professor Wilson –

Navy velvet knickers and a white shirt with puffed sleeves, a golden sash across his chest *(or something to this effect as long as he looks like he's in royal garb)*; fancy shoes; an old-fashioned hat

DON'T KISS THAT PRINCE! premièred on April 9th 2002 at Bob Jones University in Greenville SC. The cast was as follows:

PRINCE ALAN ALARMING . . . . Brandon Smith
PRINCE JONATHAN JOKESTER . . . . Daniel Hader
PRINCESS MARIA MILD . . . . Andrea Jeffcott
PRINCESS DESIREE DESIRE . . . . Heidi Roberts
PROFESSOR WHITE . . . . Joshua McSpadden

DON'T KISS THAT PRINCE!

A One-Act Realistic Fantasy

SCENE ONE

SET: *A science classroom/lab in Anytown Academy.*

(**PRINCE ALAN** *and* **PRINCE JONATHAN** *are sitting toward the back of the classroom–stage right–before the beginning of biology class.* **JONATHAN** *is poring over his notes and* **ALAN** *is watching him when the lights rise.* **ALAN** *leans back in the desk chair and crosses his arms, grinning.*)

ALAN. So, Jonathan, how long did *you* have to study for this stupid biology test?

JONATHAN. Oh, I don't know. Two or three hours, I guess.

ALAN. (*Jumping to his feet*) Two or three hours?? That is *such* a waste of time!*

(**ALAN** *reaches over and snatches* **JONATHAN**'s *notes.* **JONATHAN** *makes a brief cry of protest.* **ALAN** *flips through* **JONATHAN**'s *notes, a derisive smile on his face.*)

ALAN. (*Continued*) Good thing *I* don't have to bother with biology anymore.

(*Still in his seat,* **JONATHAN** *lunges for his notes.*)

JONATHAN. Don't tell me you didn't study for this! Professor White said this test is going to be the hardest one of the semester!

(**ALAN** *holds* **JONATHAN**'s *notes out of reach.*)

ALAN. I know.

(**JONATHAN** *slouches back in his seat with a huff and crosses his arms, frustrated that he cannot reach his notes.*)

JONATHAN. What do you mean, you know? Aren't you worried about it?

ALAN. Let's just say that I've got myself a secret weapon.

JONATHAN. *(In a loud whisper)* Alan! You don't have the test key, do you? So *that's* how you've been acing the last few tests! Unbelievable!

ALAN. Test key? Who needs a test key? *I've* got something even better!

JONATHAN. *(Skeptically)* Like what?

(**ALAN** *drops* **JONATHAN***'s notes back onto his desk.*)

ALAN. Maria.

(**JONATHAN** *gathers his papers into a neat pile again, raising an eyebrow.*)

JONATHAN. Maria? You mean, nerdy Princess Maria? What kind of secret weapon is that?

(**ALAN** *wanders over to the lab countertop and picks up a test tube. He holds it to one eye and looks up at the ceiling lights through the bottom of the tube.*)

ALAN. An excellent one when she's acing the one class I'm failing. The one class that I need to *not* fail in order to keep my perfect 4.0 and get accepted into "Harvard."

(*He says "Harvard" with a distinguished, east coast accent.*)

JONATHAN. Oh, I get it! So that's the reason you two have been spending so much time together lately!

ALAN. Duh! You didn't think it was because I actually *liked* her, did you? Come on, Jonathan! As my cousin, I would expect more brain cells than that from you.

(**ALAN** *puts the test tube back down in the rack and leans against the counter, crossing his arms.* **ALAN** *runs a hand through his hair.*)

ALAN *(continued)* I mean, let's think about this one! Sharp, suave, good-looking Prince Alan with a wallflower like Princess Maria? What *doesn't* belong in this picture?

JONATHAN. I should have known. Alan, you are such a con artist! But how did you get *her* to help *you*?

ALAN. That, my friend, was the easiest part of all! All I had to do was gaze into her eyes and speak sweet words of science, and her nerdy, little mind was captivated. Since then, my biology grade has been going up, up, up and my study time has become essentially, zip!

(**JONATHAN** *leans back in his chair and begins looking over his notes again.*)

JONATHAN. Humph. Well, sounds like a good deal for you.

(*He shoots* **ALAN** *a glance out of the corner of his eye.*)

JONATHAN *(Continued. Slyly)* You know…since you seem to be so…involved with stealing smarts from Maria, maybe I should take Desiree off your hands. Since you're so *busy* and all.

ALAN. Yeah. Dream on, Jonathan!

(**MARIA** *enters the room. Both boys cast a glance at her,—* **JONATHAN** *over his shoulder and* **ALAN** *with a casual turn of the head—look at each other, and then try to suppress their grins.* **MARIA**, *suddenly self-conscious, licks her lips, walks past them to the front of the room and puts her books down on her desk.* **ALAN**, *having conquered his smirk, stands and saunters over to her. He places a hand over the notes she has just opened and leans forward to talk to her. She looks up slowly with wide eyes and fluttery breath.*)

ALAN. *(Continued)* Maria! Hey. I'm so glad you're here. I've been waiting to talk to you.

MARIA. Me? You've…been waiting to talk t-to me?

ALAN. None other. Mind if I sit here?

(**MARIA** *shakes her head emphatically as he slides into the seat beside her.*)

ALAN. *(Continued)* So...you ready for the test?

(**MARIA** *opens her mouth to respond.* **ALAN** *mockingly smacks a hand to his head.*)

ALAN. *(Continued)* No, wait. Don't answer that. It's a dumb question. You're *always* ready for a test. You know, I'll bet you're the smartest girl in this entire class.

(**MARIA** *blushes and looks down at her feet. It is obvious that she has a crush on him. In the back,* **JONATHAN** *grins and turns back to his notes. Other students are beginning to filter into the room.* **MARIA**, *red-faced, looks down at her own notes and begins to study, conscious of* **ALAN** *peering at them over her shoulder.*)

ALAN. *(Continued)* So...it's going to be a hard test, huh?

(**MARIA** *nods and rubs her eyes, shooting occasional shy glances at* **ALAN**.)

MARIA. I think so. I...I was up half the night studying for it.

ALAN. Well, I guess that's good for both of us.

(**MARIA** *looks over at him puzzled.* **ALAN** *clears his throat and continues speaking.*)

ALAN. *(Continued)* You know, I really admire a girl with your diligence. I think intelligence is so much more attractive than good looks, don't you think?

MARIA. Oh...well I...I really don't know....But if...if you think so...

ALAN. *(Low, alluring voice)* I do.

(*While* **ALAN** *and* **MARIA** *have been talking, students have been entering the room. They now are all studying frantically. The bell rings just as* **PROFESSOR WHITE** *enters with a stack of papers in his arms. The class, except for* **ALAN**, *lets out audible groans and grumbles.* **WHITE** *sets the stack on the desk with a thud and a smile.*)

PROFESSOR WHITE. Oh, come on now, people. You knew this was coming. Now please clear your desks for the test.

(The students begin to reluctantly put their notes away. ALAN is sitting straight up, confidently looking around the room with a carefree, smug smile.)

ALAN. Yeah, what's wrong with you people? *I*, for one, am ready for this test! Bring it on!

(MARIA looks over and gives him a wondering look. ALAN notices and smiles back charmingly. She takes a deep breath, embarrassed, and looks down, a shy smile slowly coming to her face.)

PROFESSOR WHITE. I'm sure we're all very happy for you, Mr. Alarming. But let me remind you *not* to speak out in class…Now, before I hand out your tests, I want to remind you that science fair projects are due tomorrow by five.

ALAN. *(Suddenly alarmed)* Science fair projects?! What science fair projects??

PROFESSOR WHITE. *(Ignoring him)* You need to have them set up no later than five-thirty for the science fair. And remember, first prize is $500 and an A in the class, so make sure you get those projects done and done well.

(Tests in hand, he walks to the back of the class, stage right, and begins to hand them out, placing them upside-down on each student's desk. ALAN puts his head down on the desk and covers his face with his arms.)

ALAN. I cannot believe this!

(MARIA turns around and looks at him wide-eyed.)

MARIA. Didn't you remember? We were supposed to have been working on our projects for the last month!

ALAN. Well then, how come *I* didn't know about it?

PROFESSOR WHITE. No more talking, please. The test is being passed out.

(ALAN covers his face again.)

ALAN. Good idea. I think I'll do the same.

(Suddenly, ALAN sits up, fidgeting nervously in his seat.)

Oh man! What am I gonna do?

MARIA. Shh, Alan! We aren't supposed to be talking now!

(**PROFESSOR WHITE** *walks by and* **MARIA** *quickly faces the front of the room, biting her lip.* **PROFESSOR WHITE** *smiles at her and places a test face-down on her desk and then turns and puts one on* **ALAN**'*s before walking to his desk.* **ALAN** *watches* **PROFESSOR WHITE** *walk back to his desk and then casts a glance at* **MARIA**. *She quickly flips her test over and begins working. He lets out a tense breath.*)

ALAN. *(To himself)* All right. No sense in panicking yet. I just need to use my head.

(*He closes his eyes and takes a moment to regain his composure. A slow, sly smile creeps onto his face and he reopens his eyes, looking at* **MARIA** *with interest.*)

ALAN. *(Continued. In a loud whisper)* Hey...Maria! How about going out for ice cream at the Gazebo after we ace this test?

(**MARIA** *looks up at him quickly, unsure yet hopeful. He gives her an encouraging smile.*)

MARIA. Alan, I...I'd love to!

ALAN. All right, then. It's a date.

(**ALAN** *confidently flips over his test and picks up his pencil.* **MARIA** *watches him for a moment adoringly, then starts, remembering her test, takes a deep breath, and begins working again.* **ALAN** *shoots a quick glance at her out of the corner of his eye, then at the teacher. Seeing no one looking, he peers over her shoulder at her answers to the first few questions, and then hurriedly scribbles the answers on his own paper with a smug grin. The LIGHTS fade.*)

End of Scene.

SCENE TWO

SET: The Gazebo, an old-fashioned ice cream parlor.

(**ALAN** *and* **MARIA** *are sitting at a little table for two downstage in the parlor.* **ALAN** *is wolfing down a hot fudge sundae while* **MARIA** *sips on a shake.*)

MARIA. *(In quiet excitement)*...and so all I have left to do is find a frog, and my project is finished! It's been a lot of work, but it's been fun, too. I really am excited about the fair this year. I was...kind of hoping my project would win. I could use the five hundred dollars to put towards college. Do you think I have a chance?

ALAN. *(Glumly)* More of a chance than I've got.

(**ALAN** *leans forward on his elbow, gazing into her eyes, his sundae forgotten.*)

ALAN. *(Continued)* Your project sounds great. I wish finding a frog was the only thing *I* had left! Maria, what am I going to do? Our science projects are due tomorrow night and I haven't even started! I cannot believe I totally forgot about them. I must not have been thinking. My grade is doomed!

MARIA. Oh, Alan, I'm sorry. I wish there was something I could do...

(She pauses, biting her lip, deep in thought.)

I...I've worked so hard on my project. Weeks and weeks, in fact. But...

ALAN. Yes?

MARIA. Well...I know how much you need an A in the class. You know, to go to Harvard and all. And I...I suppose I can think of another project to do quickly before tomorrow. You really need the A, and...I...well, I guess I don't. Not really, anyway.

ALAN. *(Slowly; in amazement)* Maria...are you offering me your science project?

MARIA. Well, I...I...yeah, I guess I am.

ALAN. Oh, no. No. I couldn't take it from you. After all, you've worked so hard. You said so yourself. But I think you are absolutely *wonderful* to offer it to me.

(**ALAN** *smiles winningly at her and reaches out to clasp her hands in his.* **MARIA** *quickly draws her hands back in embarrassment, wetting her lips.*)

MARIA. Oh, well, that's…that's okay, Alan. I…I *want* to help you. And I really do want you to have my science project. It will be much easier for me to come up with a quick project than for you. After all, you *do* have that big basketball game tonight against Somewhere High, and I…I didn't…have any plans for tonight anyways.

ALAN. Maria, I…How can I ever thank you?

(**ALAN** *reaches for her hand again and quickly plants a kiss on it.* **MARIA** *shyly pulls her hands away, turning red. She wrings her hands together in nervous embarrassment.*)

MARIA. It's no big deal. Really.

ALAN. *(Suavely)* Well, *I* think it is. And I'll be over your house tonight to pick up the project. Will that be all right?

MARIA. Yes, that…that would be fine. I should be—

(**MARIA** *is interrupted as* **DESIREE** *strolls in, stage right.*)

DESIREE. Why, Prince Alan! Long time, no see. I was beginning to think you had forgotten about me. *(Coldly; to* **MARIA***)* Oh. Hello, Maria. *(To* **ALAN***)* Alan, you haven't forgotten about our date, have you? You promised to take me out to dinner tonight after the big game. I hope our plans haven't…changed.

(**DESIREE** *looks down dismissively over her shoulder at* **MARIA**.)

ALAN. Look, Desiree, we'll talk later, okay?

DESIREE. *(Indignant)* But Alan!

ALAN. *(Giving her a meaningful look)* I said, later. I'm sort of *busy* right now.

DESIREE. So I see. Well, if you ever *happen* to decide you finally want to talk, you know where to find me. Just don't expect me to wait around long.

(She turns and flounces out, stage right. **JONATHAN** *enters stage right as* **DESIREE** *exits. She brushes past him hard and fast.* **JONATHAN** *nearly falls over, catches himself, then gazes longingly after* **DESIREE** *with a sigh. He takes a seat at the nearby table, pulls a magazine from his back pocket, leans back in the chair, and begins to read, keeping one eye on* **ALAN** *and* **MARIA**. **ALAN** *leans forward in his chair and sighs in relief, resting his face in his hands.)*

MARIA. I…take it you two are still dating?

ALAN. She seems to think so anyway.

MARIA. Well, I'm sure you don't need me around to make it even more uncomfortable for you. I need to be going anyway. I…have a science project to work on.

ALAN. *(Genuinely)* Hey, thanks again, Maria.

(She returns his smile with only a hint of regret and exits, stage right. **JONATHAN** *watches her leave and then jumps up and races excitedly over to* **ALAN**.*)*

JONATHAN. So, did you get it??

*(**ALAN** pushes his half-eaten sundae away and leans back in his chair, looking bored.)*

ALAN. Let's just say, "Piece of cake."

JONATHAN. No way. No way! I can't believe it! You actually got her to give up her *science project* to you?

ALAN. *(Not quite so cocky)* What can I say? I'm good. And I think she's got it for me bad.

*(**ALAN** shakes his head with a sad half-smile.)*

Poor girl.

JONATHAN. I saw Desiree run out of here a minute ago, huffing and puffing. What gives?

ALAN. Oh. Her. She just about ruined everything. She

asked about our date tonight, and I didn't want to mess things up with Maria, so I had to give Desiree the brush off. She's probably pretty mad about it right now, but she'll live.

JONATHAN. Yeah, I guess you're right. Man, I *still* can't believe you got Maria's science project! So, what's it about? Plants? Solar energy?

ALAN. Even better. This project is so unusual it's sure to get me my first-place A.

JONATHAN. Oh yeah? So what's this grand and glorious project about?

ALAN. Frogs!

JONATHAN. *(Looking alarmed)* Frogs? What do you mean, frogs?

ALAN. Just what I said. The project is about frogs. And it's almost entirely done, too. All I need to do is get the frog.

(**JONATHAN** *smacks a hand to his forehead.*)

JONATHAN. You idiot! Where do you expect to get a frog? Don't you know that there *aren't* any more frogs in Anytown?!

ALAN. *(Suddenly alarmed)* What do you mean, there aren't any more frogs in Anytown?

JONATHAN. Don't you remember anything from history class, Alan? Remember the seventies? When all those princesses got caught up in that...hogwash...about kissing frogs to get princes? There hasn't been a frog in Anytown since!

ALAN. But...but Maria wouldn't do the project if she couldn't find a frog!

JONATHAN. Well, I guess you could probably find some a few towns over in Elsewhere, but there isn't enough time now. The big game's tonight, remember?

ALAN. How could I forget?

JONATHAN. Sometimes I wonder the same thing.

(**ALAN** *jumps out of his seat and begins to pace.*)

ALAN. Jonathan, this is horrible! What am I going to do??

(**JONATHAN** *reopens his magazine and answers without looking up.*)

JONATHAN. Maybe you should do your own science fair project.

ALAN. What, are you crazy? No, there's no time for that! But there must be something I can do…

(**JONATHAN** *flips a few pages of his magazine, reaches for* **ALAN***'s half-eaten sundae, and takes a big bite.*)

JONATHAN. Good luck.

ALAN. Oh, man. I am in *big* trouble.

(**ALAN** *begins pacing faster.*)

ALAN *(Continued)* Okay. Okay. I've got to think. There's got to be a way out. My grade is depending on this project! Now…how can I get a frog… ?

(**JONATHAN***'s eyes, still on his magazine, suddenly light up. He casts a sly smile at* **ALAN**.*)

JONATHAN. *(Casually)* Hmmm… I think I may have just figured out a way.

(**ALAN** *runs over to him and grabs him by the shirt collar, nearly knocking him out of his seat. The magazine flutters to the ground.*)

ALAN. What?? How??

JONATHAN. Hey! Take it easy, Killer!

(**ALAN** *lets go of him and takes his seat in an agitated manner.* **JONATHAN** *straightens his collar indignantly.*)

JONATHAN *(Continued)* That's better.

(**JONATHAN** *stands up and reaches down to pick up his magazine.*)

JONATHAN *(Continued)* Now, as I was saying, I think I know how you can get a frog before tomorrow night.

ALAN. Well?? Tell me!

JONATHAN. *(With a grin)* What's it worth to you?

(**ALAN** *shoves his chair out quickly as he stands, scraping* *it against the floor.)*

ALAN. Jonathan, don't play games with me. You know how important this biology grade is. My application to Harvard is sitting on my desk back at home *waiting* to be mailed. All I need is the guarantee of an A in biology and I'm set. Now tell me... how can I get a blasted frog?!

(**JONATHAN** *crosses his arms with a big smile, clearly enjoying himself and not intimidated in the least.)*

JONATHAN. Ooh, touchy. Okay, Mr. Hotshot-I Wanna-Be-A-Lawyer. I'll tell you how to get a frog. But first...let me have a date with Desiree.

ALAN. *(With a snort)* Get real, Jonathan.

JONATHAN. I am real. I want a date with Desiree, and you want a frog. I'll tell you how to get one if you tell Desiree to go out with me. Just once, that's all I'm asking.

ALAN. What makes you think I can convince her to go out with you? She's got her own mind.

JONATHAN. *(Laughing)* Desiree? A mind? Looks, yes. A personality, maybe. But a mind? Nah. Besides, she's crazy about you. She'd do anything you asked her to.

(With a smirk)

Kinda like Maria....So, is it a deal?

(**ALAN** *pauses for a moment.)*

ALAN. Fine. But only *one* date. Because after this mess with the science projects is over and I have my A, I intend to go back to dating Desiree. My reputation will *need* the boost.

JONATHAN. That's fine. I'm only asking for one.

(**JONATHAN** *walks back over to the table, pulls out a chair, and sits back down.* **ALAN** *quickly pulls out a chair and sits down as well.)*

JONATHAN *(Continued))* Now, for your frog...

ALAN. Yes?

(**JONATHAN** *reopens his magazine and flips through the pages.*)

JONATHAN. *(Slowly; tantalizingly)* Well…you remember how I said that in the seventies all those princesses got caught up in that kissing fad, thinking the frogs would turn into princes?

ALAN. Yeah. What about it?

(**JONATHAN** *continues flipping.*)

JONATHAN. Well, obviously, that didn't work. So some scientists got together to do a little research on the matter. And their findings are reported here. In this magazine.

ALAN. *(Wearily)* Jonathan, where are you going with all of this?

(**ALAN** *makes a move to stand again.*)

Look, we are wasting time sitting here talking about old news!

JONATHAN. *But* it's not *all* old news.

ALAN. Continue.

JONATHAN. As I was saying, there's an article in this magazine that gives a *new* scientific finding that's resulted from their research.

(Slowly)

They found out that something actually happens not when a princess kisses a frog, but when a prince kisses a princess he does not truly love.

ALAN. *(Starting to sound interested)* What happens?

(**JONATHAN** *stops flipping pages and holds the magazine out to* **ALAN.**)

JONATHAN. *She* turns into a frog.

(**ALAN** *grabs the magazine and scans it quickly.*)

ALAN. So all I have to do is kiss a princess I don't actually love and she'll turn into a frog?

(**JONATHAN** *leans back in his chair with a self-satisfied smirk.*)

JONATHAN. Exactly.

ALAN. *(Slowly)* Hmm…a princess I don't actually love. Well, I *guess* that means Desiree is out. So then I suppose the best choice left would have to be…

(**JONATHAN** *looks at him knowingly and nods.* **ALAN***'s eyes light up.*)

JONATHAN and **ALAN.** Maria!

(The LIGHTS fade.)

End of Scene.

SCENE THREE

SET: *Back in the science classroom/lab at the Academy (****MARIA*** *is frantically mixing chemicals, trying to trace letters for her board, and write in a log book for her project all at the same time. She accidentally drops a test tube and it shatters on the floor. She rips her safety goggles off, sets them down on the countertop, and throws herself down into a desk, her head in her hands.)*

MARIA. Why in the world did I ever give my project away? What was I thinking?? I need to win just as much as he does! Five hundred dollars is a lot of money. I could really use it, too. But now...

(**MARIA** *looks at the mess around her.*)

(Dismally) ...it looks as though I haven't got a chance.

(She slowly takes a deep breath.)

No. No, I can't give up yet. I just have to keep working.

(**MARIA** *kneels down carefully and begins picking up the shards from the broken test tube.* **DESIREE***, who has been peering in the window for the last few moments, suddenly throws the door open. It is after the basketball game and she is in her cheerleading uniform. She has a duffel bag thrown over her shoulder.)*

DESIREE. There you are. I should have *known* you'd be up here. Alan told me to give you a message.

(**MARIA** *looks up from the floor hopefully.*)

MARIA. Yes?

DESIREE. He said to tell you that he was going to be a little...late...

(Narrowing her eyes)

...coming over tonight.

(Smiling again)

We are going out to dinner to celebrate the win.

MARIA. For the science fair?

(**DESIREE** *drops the duffel bag from her shoulder onto the floor.*)

DESIREE. No, stupid. Our win over Somewhere. The basketball game, remember? Or are you so wrapped up in your own little world of science that the real world just goes right over your head?

(**MARIA** *gazes off into the distance.*)

MARIA. *(Wistfully)* The basketball game…that's right. That was tonight. Alan was telling me about that this afternoon.

(Dreamily; looking back at Desiree)

Did he play well? Alan, I mean.

DESIREE. Of course he played well. Alan *always* plays well, if you know what I mean. And *that* is exactly why I'd watch myself if I were you, Maria. Alan knows how to play the game *very* well.

(**DESIREE** *slowly circles* **MARIA** *with a smirk on her face, eyeing her clothes, her hair, and finally walking over to where her science project board is set up. She picks up a beaker filled with green liquid and studies it, a look of cruel humor in her eyes. She sets the glass down on the countertop with a bang.*)

DESIREE. *(Continued)* I mean, really? What makes you think someone like Alan would have any real interest in *you* anyway?

(**MARIA** *slowly stands, holding the bits of shattered test tube carefully in her hands.*)

MARIA. I…never expected that he would ever *like* me. I was only trying to be a friend to him. That was all.

DESIREE. Well, you can stop trying. In case you have forgotten, he has me. We've been dating for months now and I'm certainly not going to let someone like *you* ruin it for me.

(DESIREE takes a few steps closer to MARIA. MARIA steps back, looking intimidated.)

DESIREE. *(Continued. Mockingly)* Don't you know how the story goes by now, Maria? It's the handsome prince and the beautiful princess that always end up happily ever after. There just isn't any room in the picture for the ugly frog. So I suggest you get out of it. Get my drift?

(MARIA rubs her free hand against her eyes and walks past DESIREE.)

MARIA. Desiree, I don't need this right now. I've had a lot on my mind lately. Especially tonight. It's not easy trying to come up with a science project in one night.

DESIREE. Well…isn't that too bad? Perhaps next time you should plan ahead a little better.

(MARIA walks over to the trash can and dumps the pieces of glass in with gusto.)

MARIA. I *did* plan ahead. But something…unexpected came up.

DESIREE. As I said, you should have planned ahead better. *My* project is all done. And as a matter of fact, so is Alan's. And if *he* can find the time with *his* social life, I'm sure you had plenty of time to work on yours.

(With a smirk)

Since…you have no social life. Well, Alan's waiting for me. I'll let you get back to your work.

(DESIREE walks past MARIA and condescendingly pats her on the cheek.)

DESIREE. *(Continued)* Don't blow anything up now, dear. Toodles!

(DESIREE exits. MARIA watches her leave, red-faced. As the door slams shut, MARIA explodes in a cry of frustration.)

MARIA. *(Close to tears)* Ooh, that girl! She makes me so angry!

(She stomps back over to the counter and picks up the safety goggles and readjusts them on her head. In a flurry of activity, she races to the cupboard, pulls out another test tube, walks back over to her project, and picks up the beaker of green liquid. Standing behind the counter, she holds the test tube up to the beaker again, facing the audience, and is just about to pour when she pauses. Her face falls. Swallowing hard, she sets the test tube in a rack and the beaker down beside it. Slowly she guides herself into a desk.)

MARIA *(Continued)* No, she... she *couldn't* be right.

*(**MARIA** pauses, biting her lip.)*

(In a whisper) But what if she is? What if he *is* just using me?

*(**MARIA** looks back to her science project board, her eyes widening in sudden revelation. She breathes in sharply.)*

It must be true. Alan, he...he never really liked me. He only wanted my project! How could I have been so blind?

(She takes her glasses from her face and puts her head down on her arms. After a moment, she jumps up, gathers her board and materials, and runs from the room. The LIGHTS fade.)

End of Scene.

SCENE FOUR

SET: *The science classroom the following night, ten minutes before the science fair begins. The students' desks have been replaced by rows of tables on which various projects and boards are displayed around the room. Students are milling about, talking excitedly and putting finishing touches on their displays.)*

LIGHTING: *The lights come up brightly on the entire set, but as the scene begins, the stage LIGHTS on the surrounding action slowly dim so that a dim SPOTLIGHT on* **ALAN** *and* **JONATHAN** *becomes visible at center stage. The LIGHTING on the rest of the set should be dimmer, but not dark.*

*(***"ALAN's"*** *frog project is displayed prominently, at center stage in the first row. It is clearly the best-looking display in the room. His name is written in bold letters underneath the title of his project: "Can Frogs Feel Pain Too?" A stuffed frog sits in front of his display. As the LIGHTS come up,* **ALAN** *is standing in front of his board, looking around nervously.* **JONATHAN** *enters from stage right and strolls over to* **ALAN***. He circles* **ALAN***'s display, admiring it.)*

JONATHAN. Hey, man! Great board! That'll really impress the judges. But where's the...you know...*(Lowering his voice)*...the frog?

*(***ALAN***'s brow furrows nervously; his mouth tightens, but he doesn't say anything. He keeps looking around the room.)*

JONATHAN. *(Continued)* Uh-oh. You don't have a frog yet, do you?

*(***ALAN** *runs a hand through his hair nervously, trying to sound calm.)*

ALAN. Don't...don't worry. I'll get one. It's all under control.

*(***JONATHAN** *crosses his arms and leans back against the*

table.)

JONATHAN. *(Skeptically)* Uh-huh. So…what happened to Maria? You obviously got the project from her last night. Why didn't you just do it then?

(**ALAN** *begins pacing in front of his board.*)

ALAN. *(Tightly)* I…I couldn't. She…she wasn't in when I went to her house to get the project. Her mom said she hadn't seen her all day, so I just took the project and left.

JONATHAN. So what are you going to do? The judging starts in five minutes!

ALAN. I know, I know. I've got to find Maria.

(**MARIA** *enters with her project unobtrusively from stage right, crosses the room by going behind the other projects, and sets her board up in the back corner of the room, stage left. It is obvious that her board has been hastily put together. She works quickly, her head down in shame. Both* **JONATHAN** *and* **ALAN** *look up quickly when she enters. Their eyes follow her.* **JONATHAN** *gives* **ALAN** *a nudge.*)

JONATHAN. Hey, now's your chance! She's here! Go get your frog, Prince Charming!

(**ALAN** *straightens and turns toward her. He hesitates for a moment.*)

JONATHAN. *(Continued. With a confused laugh)* What's wrong, Slick? Cold feet?

(*A strange look crosses* **ALAN**'s *face—a mixture of eagerness, anxiety, and regret. His eyes are still on* **MARIA**.)

ALAN. Jonathan?

JONATHAN. Yeah?

(**ALAN** *turns back around to face* **JONATHAN**.)

ALAN. *(In a low voice)* What happens if she *doesn't* turn into a frog?

JONATHAN. *(Taken aback)* Oh. Well, according to the article, she *should* turn into a frog. That's what's supposed to happen when a prince kisses a princess he doesn't really love, right?

(**JONATHAN** *chuckles uncomfortably.* **ALAN** *nods somewhat reluctantly.*)

ALAN. *(Quiet; unsure)* Right. So long as he doesn't really love her…

(**ALAN***'s voice trails off. He pauses, then firmly shakes his head, looking resolute, takes a deep breath, and takes a few steps toward* **MARIA**.)

JONATHAN. *(Calling out after him)* Hey! What about my date with Desiree?

ALAN. You can have her!

(**ALAN** *crosses the stage toward* **MARIA**, *who is busy plugging in an extension cord. The SPOTLIGHT follows him, leaving* **JONATHAN** *in the semi-darkness. Another SPOTLIGHT rises on* **MARIA***'s corner.*

Before reaching her, **ALAN** *pauses and watches her struggle with the cord for a moment, a concerned look crossing his face. He leans over and taps* **MARIA** *on the shoulder. She stands up slowly and turns to face him. The two SPOTLIGHTS become one. The two begin to talk out of earshot of the audience, the SPOTLIGHT still on them.*

Another SPOTLIGHT rises on stage right where **JONATHAN** *is standing talking to* **DESIREE***. She is in front of her science project, a cutesy board with rainbows, hearts, and flowers on it. In front of the board are three potted flowers. She is standing with her arms crossed, glaring over at* **ALAN** *and* **MARIA**. **JONATHAN** *is leaning back against the counter casually.*)

DESIREE. *(Glaring at them)* Oooh, those two! They make me so mad I could just spit!

JONATHAN. *(Trying to sound suave)* What's the problem?

(**DESIREE** *whirls around to face* **JONATHAN**, *her hands on her hips, indignantly.*)

DESIREE. I just don't understand him! How could he seriously be interested in that little brainiac?

JONATHAN. Guess she must have some sort of magnetic attraction. Get it? Science fair? Magnetic attraction?

(**JONATHAN** *chuckles at his own joke, but* **DESIREE** *just turns and gives him a dirty look.* **JONATHAN** *stops mid-laugh and grimaces.*)

JONATHAN. *(Continued)* So what makes you so sure he's interested in her?

DESIREE. *(Her eyes narrowing)* Trust me. I can tell. Besides, at dinner last night all he could talk about was *Maria*.

(Mockingly sounding like **ALAN***)*

"I can't stay long. I have to stop by *Maria's*." "It's been great having *Maria's* help in biology." "Desiree, you don't think Maria is a complete nerd, do you?"

(**DESIREE** *makes a face.*)

It makes me sick. Absolutely sick. It's almost as if he's actually starting to have feelings for the little toadstool. What in the world is his problem?

(**JONATHAN** *shakes his head and sighs, casually reaching into his back pocket and pulling out his paper crown. He carefully unfolds it and places it on his head at a rakish tilt.*)

JONATHAN. Who knows? My cousin has never really had very good taste in women.

(**DESIREE***'s eyes suddenly light up with comprehension. She turns to face* **JONATHAN**, *a new light of appreciation in her eyes.*)

DESIREE. Cousin? Alan's your…cousin? *(Suddenly interested)* Is that right?

(**DESIREE** *casually leans back against the display table beside him, giving him her full attention and a flirty smile.*)

DESIREE. *(Continued)* I never realized you two were…

related. But now that you've mentioned it, I can sorta see the resemblance.

(**DESIREE** *leans in closer to him, studying his face and batting her eyes coyly.*)

You *do* have the same stately nose.

(**JONATHAN** *grins, enjoying her attention.* **PROFESSOR WHITE** *enters the classroom, stage right.*)

The SPOTLIGHTS on the two couples fade as the LIGHTS brighten on the entire set. The scene continues. **PROFESSOR WHITE** *walks to the center of the room.*

PROFESSOR WHITE. May I have your attention, please? The judging is about to begin. If I could have you all please exit the room at this time, we'll get started immediately. Thank you.

(*He exits stage right. The students start filing excitedly out of the room via stage right. A few last-minute adjustments are given to boards and displays.* **JONATHAN** *and* **DESIREE** *do not move right away; the rest of the students file past them.* **ALAN** *and* **MARIA**, *still in serious conversation, slowly walk towards the center of the room,* **ALAN** *in the lead. As he approaches his frogless display, his head jerks up as though having just noticed it. He looks around frantically for a moment.* **MARIA** *stares at him as though he has gone crazy.* **ALAN** *stops at his display with a halt,* **MARIA** *nearly running into him.* **JONATHAN** *observes him aloud from stage right as* **DESIREE** *makes a motion to leave.*)

JONATHAN. *(To* **DESIREE**; *suspenseful, eager)* Uh-oh. I think he's gonna do it!

(**DESIREE** *looks back at* **JONATHAN** *over her shoulder.*)

DESIREE. *(Suspiciously)* Do what?

JONATHAN. I think Alan's going to kiss her!

DESIREE. He's going to do *what?*!?

(**DESIREE** *whirls around and charges back into the center of the room.* **JONATHAN** *watches her speechless.*)

DESIREE. *(Continued)* Stop! Don't kiss that prince!!!

(Just as **DESIREE** *is yelling the words,* **ALAN** *leans over and quickly pecks* **MARIA** *on the cheek. She immediately turns red and takes a step back, her hand on her cheek.* **DESIREE** *stops just short of center stage.)*

MARIA. What...what was that for?

*(***ALAN** *watches her closely for several seconds. When nothing happens, he looks stunned.* **JONATHAN**, *also surprised, freezes in his place.* **DESIREE** *is the only person still in motion at this time.)*

DESIREE. *What* is going *on?* Alan Alarming, you had better explain yourself!

JONATHAN. *(Slowly; confused; looking disappointed)* She... didn't...turn into a frog.

*(***DESIREE** *whirls to face* **JONATHAN**.*)*

DESIREE. Turn into a *what?!?*

*(***ALAN** *is gazing into* **MARIA***'s eyes wonderingly.)*

ALAN. *(A whispered statement, almost to himself)* She didn't turn into a frog.

MARIA. *(Wounded)* Turn into a frog? Were you expecting me too?

ALAN. Well, I...I thought...

*(***DESIREE** *charges to center stage, breaking between the two of them.)*

DESIREE. *You* are the one who's a frog, Prince Alan!

(She grabs the stuffed frog sitting on **ALAN***'s display and hits him with it. He throws his arms up to shield the blow.* **DESIREE** *stomps out.* **ALAN** *looks down at the floor.* **JONATHAN**, *regretfully watching her storm out, turns to* **ALAN** *with a sigh.)*

JONATHAN. Sorry, man. I...I could have sworn it was true.

MARIA. *(Frustrated)* What was true?

JONATHAN. *(With a grin)* Well...they say if a handsome prince kisses a princess he doesn't really love, she'll turn into a frog. We needed a frog for this project, and there you were…

(**ALAN**'s *head jerks up in fear. He glares at* **JONATHAN** *for a long moment, then casts a worried look at* **MARIA**. **MARIA** *steps back, a hurt look on her face. There is a long pause.* **ALAN** *takes a tentative step toward* **MARIA**, *one hand reaching out to her.*)

ALAN. *(Nervously)* Maria…? I can explain.

(**MARIA** *jerks away from him.*)

MARIA. Desiree was right. You really are a toad.

(**MARIA** *brushes past* **ALAN** *and* **JONATHAN** *and exits the room, stage right.*)

End of Scene.

SCENE FIVE

SET: *The scene continues. It is one hour later. A podium has been placed at downstage right. The students are once again in the room milling around waiting for the results of the contest. The atmosphere is tense with excitement.*

(**ALAN**'s *frog project is nowhere to be seen; he is sitting in the corner next to* **MARIA**'s *board, looking at it morosely, the back of the board facing the audience.*)

ALAN. *(To himself)* I am such an idiot. What have I done?

(**JONATHAN**, *who has been admiring the displays in the back row, pops up behind* **ALAN**. *He is chomping on a bag of Doritos.*)

JONATHAN. Yep. You've made a pretty big mess of things.

(**ALAN** *turns to face* **JONATHAN** *angrily.*)

ALAN. You! This is all *your* fault!

JONATHAN. *My* fault? Look, man, I only *mentioned* the frog thing. You did this all on your own.

(**ALAN** *hangs his head. There is a brief pause.*)

ALAN. *(Quietly; with a sigh)* Jon, I…I think I really *do* like her.

JONATHAN. *(Surprised)* You do?

ALAN. She…she did so much to help me. And the whole time, I…I was a complete jerk to her. She…cared about me. And I took advantage of that. Now I doubt if she'll ever even speak to me again. What do I do?

(**JONATHAN** *shrugs, still chomping on his chips.*)

JONATHAN. Give her the five hundred bucks, keep your A, and go to Harvard?

(**ALAN** *shakes his head and looks at his feet, a pained look in his eyes.*)

ALAN. No. I can't.

(*He looks up at* **JONATHAN**.)

ALAN. *(Continued)* I don't deserve an A. *Or* first place for her project. It's all a lie, Jonathan.

(With a quiet sigh)

And Harvard's not worth it.

JONATHAN. Hmmm. Well, I don't know what to tell you.

(JONATHAN looks over to stage right.)

But here comes someone with the answers...

*(He nods his head in the direction of stage right, where **MARIA** has just reentered. She holds her head high, glaring in **ALAN**'s direction for a moment. **ALAN** sinks lower in his chair. **JONATHAN** leaves **ALAN**, crossing the stage toward **MARIA** in a slow saunter. She starts walking over to her project, when **JONATHAN** stops her by stepping in front of her path.)*

JONATHAN. Hey, Maria. Hold on a minute.

*(**MARIA** tries to step around him, but he blocks her path again. She stops, crossing her arms.)*

JONATHAN *(Continued)* Look, I know that you're probably hurt right now and so mad you can't even see straight. So let me correct your vision for you.

*(**JONATHAN** reaches up and snatches her glasses from her face. She frowns and tries to swipe them back, but fails. He grabs her arm and turns her in the direction of **ALAN**, who is still sitting beside her display, his head in his hands. He looks up and sees her glaring at him, then jumps from his seat, grabs her board, and races across the back of the room and exits via stage right. **JONATHAN** pulls a chip from the bag and pops it into his mouth, chomping loudly.)*

JONATHAN *(Continued. Casually)* Maria, have you ever thought about the possibility that perhaps those new scientific findings *are* true? Maybe when a handsome prince kisses a princess he doesn't really love, she really does turn into a frog.

*(**MARIA** freezes up and gives him a cool glare. **JONATHAN** returns her stare without emotion. Suddenly, he gives her a genuine smile and offers his bag of chips to her.)*

JONATHAN *(Continued)* But...you *didn't* turn into a frog.... Chip?

(**MARIA**'s *eyes fall to the floor and her face softens as her mind registers this information.* **JONATHAN** *watches her, digging through the bag for another chip.* **MARIA**'s *eyes flicker over to the place* **ALAN** *had been sitting, and then quickly back to* **JONATHAN**.)

MARIA. *(Unsure)* No. It...it can't be true. There's no way...

(**JONATHAN** *grins at her as he crumples up his empty bag of chips.*)

JONATHAN. *(Interrupting her)* Don't you believe in fairy tales?

MARIA. I guess so. It's just that...I usually end up playing the frog rather than the beautiful princess.

(**JONATHAN** *plucks the crown off his head and stuffs it in his back pocket with the empty chip bag.*)

JONATHAN. Well, you're not the frog this time. And it's too bad. That would have been exciting to watch.

(**MARIA** *rolls her eyes and* **JONATHAN** *raises his arms up in self-defense.*)

JONATHAN. *(Continued)* Hey, relax! It was only a joke!

MARIA. Right.

(*She lets out a breath of air.* **ALAN** *reenters the room at stage right with her board. He is furtively shielding another object in his arms. He walks over to the place where* **MARIA**'s *display had been and puts the board back on the table, the back of it facing the audience. He then places the hidden object underneath the table.* **MARIA** *follows him with her eyes, confused.*)

MARIA *(Continued. Slowly; with a hopeful smile)* Well...I guess it couldn't hurt to give him another chance. *(To* **JONATHAN***)* Thank you.

JONATHAN. Hey, don't thank me. Just go over there and turn that sorry toad into a prince again.

(**MARIA** *smiles genuinely and begins walking toward*

ALAN, *who is pacing nervously in front of her display.* **PROFESSOR WHITE** *enters the room at the same time, stopping at downstage right beside the podium.*)

PROFESSOR WHITE. May I have your attention? Your attention, please.

(*He waits for the room to quiet down. The students and* **JONATHAN** *move to the center of the room to hear the announcement.* **ALAN** *and* **MARIA** *remain upstage, stage left, talking.* **MARIA** *walks up to* **ALAN** *tentatively.* **ALAN** *eagerly meets her.*)

MARIA. Alan, we need to talk.

ALAN. I...I know.

PROFESSOR WHITE. At this time, I would like to announce the winners of this year's science fair.

(*There is an excited buzz in the room.* **ALAN** *reaches for* **MARIA**'s *hand.* **MARIA** *smiles at him and does not draw her hand away immediately.*)

ALAN. (*Quiet and genuine, though quickly spoken*) Maria, I am so sorry.

PROFESSOR WHITE. First, for third place...This year's third place prize goes to Princess Rebekah Sonora.

(*The students clap and cheer as a perky little girl bounces to the front of the room to receive her ribbon.*)

MARIA. It's all right, Alan. I'm not angry with you.

ALAN. (*Surprised*) You're...you're not?

(**MARIA** *shakes her head and smiles, drawing her hand away.*)

MARIA. No.

(**ALAN** *looks around the room nervously, avoiding her gaze. He blows out a deep breath.*)

ALAN. (*Hesitantly*) Well, Maria...there's...there's something else you need to know...Something you *should* be angry with me about.

MARIA. Yes?

PROFESSOR WHITE. *(With a broad smile)* Second place this year once again goes to Prince Chester Rumsfield.

(The clapping of the students is not as enthusiastic this time as a snobby-looking boy stands and strolls up to the podium to accept his ribbon, an arrogant smile on his face.)

ALAN. *(Continuing hesitantly)* Well, see, I...I cheated off your biology tests—

MARIA. I know.

ALAN. ...but you must believe me when I say I'm so sorry. I just—you *knew?*

MARIA. Well, I kind of figured *something* was going on when you started sitting next to me for every test. *And* kept getting the same grade I got...

*(**ALAN** looks down at his feet in shame.)*

ALAN. I know...I know. It was rotten of me to use you that way.

(After a moment, he slowly looks back up at her.)

Do you think there's anything I can do to make it up to you?

MARIA. You...you don't have to. I forgive you. Besides, it's kind of too late for that anyway.

ALAN. But I *want* to make it up to you...

*(As the words come out of his mouth, **ALAN** looks up at the **PROFESSOR**, who is reaching for the first-prize ribbon. A smile slowly begins to appear on **ALAN**'s face and an eager look in his eye.)*

ALAN *(Continued)* And I think I know how.

PROFESSOR WHITE. And now for first place. By the unanimous vote of all four of our judges, we would like to present this year's first place prize to...Princess Maria Mild.

*(The students turn around to look at **MARIA** with big smiles, clapping enthusiastically. **MARIA**'s mouth drops open and she turns to look at the **PROFESSOR** with*

incredulity. **ALAN** *is grinning hopefully as he turns* **MARIA***'s board around to face her and the audience. It is the frog project, her name now prominently replacing his own.)*

MARIA. But, Alan, how...? When did you...?

ALAN. *(With a grin)* And that's not all...

(**ALAN** *reaches under the table and pulls out a small terrarium. In the box is a big, fat frog.* **MARIA***'s eyes widen.)*

MARIA. A frog! But...but where did you find one?

(**ALAN** *smirks down at the frog.)*

ALAN. Well, *actually* it wasn't very hard. All I had to do was give Desiree a big kiss and...

(A smile lights **MARIA***'s face and she gives* **ALAN** *a big hug.* **PROFESSOR WHITE** *makes his way through the students and pins a blue ribbon on* **MARIA***'s display. He taps her on the shoulder and holds out an envelope.* **MARIA** *takes it reverently, looking up at the professor with big eyes.)*

PROFESSOR WHITE. Alan came to me a little while ago and admitted to stealing your science project and cheating on the biology tests. He was very determined to make it up to you, though. What he did was wrong, and he will have to pay the penalty for it, but I hope you'll be able to find it in your heart to forgive him. *(With a kind smile)* He *did* try to make things right in the end.

MARIA. *(To* **PROFESSOR WHITE***)* Yes. I guess he did. *(To* **ALAN***)* Well, it's about time you turned back into a prince, Alan Alarming.

(**MARIA** *smiles as he looks down at his feet, embarrassed.)*

MARIA *(Continued)* Maybe with a little practice we'll turn you into a Prince Charming yet!

(Lights fade.)

End of Scene.

END OF PLAY

PROP LIST

Textbooks, notebooks, pencils, pens, paper, etc: for the students
Test tubes, test tube racks, and beakers: for the science lab
Stack of tests: for Professor White
A hot fudge sundae: for Alan
A milkshake cup: for Maria
A nature magazine: for Jonathan
A cheerleading duffel bag: for Desiree
Science fair project boards and displays: for each student *(Specific ones listed)*

   Desiree's – flower project; board decorated with flowers, hearts, and rainbows

   Alan's – frog project; board decorated in reds, yellows, and greens; well done

   Maria's – chemical project; last minute, hastily put together, black and white

A stuffed frog: for Alan's display
A bag of Doritos: for Jonathan
A real frog *(or at least, a real-looking fake frog)* in a clear plastic box: for the display
First, second, and third place ribbons
An envelope

COSTUME LIST

Note: This play is a modern-day twist on a fairy tale myth. Therefore, although the costumes are contemporary, each student wears a crown at all times *(with the exception of Jonathan)*. The crowns should fit each character's personality. The teacher, however, dresses in traditional royal garb. Some suggestions for student dress and Professor White's dress are given below:

Prince Alan Alarming –
Jeans or khaki pants and a polo shirt; stylish; large *(but not clownishly oversized)* gold crown

Prince Jonathan Jokester –
Jeans and a T-shirt; tennis shoes; paper or thin cardboard crown *(usually stuffed in his back pocket)*

Princess Maria Mild –
A casual, homely, earth-tone or cobalt blue dress or skirt and shirt set; boring shoes; tiny, plain crown; glasses; no makeup

Princess Desiree Desire –
<u>Scenes 2 & 4</u>: Flashy red dress or red shirt and denim skirt; high heels; ruby-studded gold crown; meticulously applied makeup; fake nails painted red

<u>Scene 3</u>: Red and white cheerleading outfit; white tennis shoes; red face paint on one cheek that says "Go Team" or something to that effect

Professor White –
<u>Male</u>: Purple velvet knickers and a white shirt with puffed sleeves, a golden sash across his chest *(or something to this effect as long as he looks like he's in royal garb)*; fancy shoes; a crown and scepter; tiny gold reading glasses

<u>Female</u>: Old-fashioned bodice gown with train; fur-trimmed hoodless cape; ornate crown; scepter

The Committee Meeting

A Comedy for Five Women in One Act
By Joellen K. Bland

5f / interior
Sue and her committee get together to plan the church congregational dinner-meeting. While she tries to guide the discussion - often with the aid of a whistle to restore order - Amy prattles, Edith complains, Doris preaches and Mary amiably agrees with just about everything. They willingly offer comments, ideas and suggestions, but when they are asked to assume responsibility, each responds with a prompt excuse for not accepting, and volunteers the time and services of someone else.

Please visit our website **bakersplays.com** for complete descriptions and licensing information

The Babysitter

Laurie Woodward 5f / interior

Eyes at the window," warns the Ouija board, and Karen realizes that she and her friends are being watched! Searching the house, she discovers there is no child to babysit! An old newspaper clipping reveals that the Williams' baby daughter died mysteriously ten years ago. The terrifying finale reveals who the Williams are, and what is in store for the babysitter! A thriller for all lovers of things that go bump in the night!

Please visit our website **bakersplays.com** for complete descriptions and licensing information

www.ingramcontent.com/pod-product-compliance
Lightning Source LLC
Chambersburg PA
CBHW071841290426
44109CB00017B/1895